LOST
IN A CAVE

Aurora Colón García
Illustrated by Becky Radtke

Rigby
A Harcourt Achieve Imprint

www.Rigby.com
1-800-531-5015

To all my wonderful supportive friends, especially Sylvia Suárez, who has been my safe haven in sad and happy times. Sincere and heartfelt appreciation to the great Bruno and Rose Vallin for believing in me and for their support.

Literacy by Design Leveled Readers: *Lost in a Cave*

Contents

The Adventure Begins

The Cruz family had really been enjoying their first few days of vacation at Winding River Campground in the Texas hill country. They'd taken nature walks, played ball games, told scary stories around the campfire, and cooled off in the campground's sparkling pool, complete with water slide—what a great vacation!

Another thing that made this vacation so great, especially for Dora, was that her eighteen-year-old cousin, Sylvia, was working as a junior park ranger at nearby Great Cavern Park. Sylvia had already joined the family for cookouts and had taken Dora, Omar, and Carlos to the ranger station where she worked, and there they were able to meet some of the other park rangers, who told them about the different activities the park sponsored.

That evening the three children excitedly told their parents about some of the activities.

"You can go backpacking in the hills and search for fossils," said Omar. "You do know that dinosaurs once roamed these very hills, don't you?"

"Or you can go on a trail ride in a covered wagon and set up camp for one night along the river, just like early settlers did," added Carlos.

"Or . . . you can explore Great Cavern, probably the coolest cave in the whole world," exclaimed Dora, "and Sylvia is one of the guides!"

Mom and Dad liked seeing this kind of enthusiasm in their children, so Dad said, "Why don't you each pick the one activity you really want to do and we'll go sign up for them tomorrow morning?"

Omar, Carlos, and Dora drifted off to sleep, knowing what they wanted to do, and then changing their minds, then changing them back again . . . and again . . . and again.

The next morning the Cruz family—all minds made up—walked to the ranger station.

Omar and Carlos both wanted to go on the covered wagon trail ride. Omar thought it sounded a little more exciting than a fossil hunt, and Dad had never been in a covered wagon before, so he thought he'd go along with the boys, while Mom would join

Dora on her adventure. And, of course, that would be exploring Great Cavern, the coolest cave in the world!

Dad, Omar, and Carlos hurriedly went back to the campground to get their gear ready—the trail ride would begin at noon—and Mom and Dora stayed to talk with Sylvia and Eddy, the young ranger who would lead the exploration of Great Cavern.

"Please read this information carefully," Eddy told Mom and Dora as he handed each of them two lists—one telling them what supplies they'd need and the other providing safety rules.

Suddenly Mom turned to Dora and said, "Oh . . . I just thought of something—what are we going to do with Chico? We can't leave him alone all that time, and I know your father and the boys won't be able to take him on the trail ride."

"Can't we bring him with us?" Dora asked her mom as she looked hopefully at Eddy. "I'll watch him, and we'll put him on his leash while we're in the cave."

"You can bring Chico, but it will be your responsibility to keep him out of trouble," Eddy answered.

"I promise that he'll be the best dog in the world, and I'll watch him every single second," Dora answered as she smiled at Eddy and her mother.

2

The Storm

Bright and early the next morning, Mom, Dora, and Chico joined Eddy and Sylvia at the ranger station, where Eddy introduced them to the other first-time cave explorers—Ric, Lucy, and Felipe. He then went over the rules one more time, making sure everyone in the group understood them and all backpacks contained the necessary items. He supplied each explorer with a hard hat that had a headlamp attached to it, and they were off.

About 20 minutes into the hike, the sky suddenly grew darker, and buckets of water drenched the earth, catching everyone by surprise.

"So much for a forecast of partly cloudy," Eddy said as he looked around for shelter, but he almost panicked when he saw the children head for shelter under a huge oak tree. "Don't go under that tree—it's a dangerous place to be in a thunderstorm! Follow Sylvia into that cave entrance—we'll be safe there."

As Mom and Sylvia gathered the children at the cave entrance, Eddy tried to reassure himself about his choice. He knew that this wild, or unexplored, cave could be dangerous. Its narrow passageways could lead to all kinds of trouble, but for now it was the only shelter nearby, and he figured they would be OK as long as they stayed near the cave's entrance.

The rush of everyone scrambling to get into the cave sent Felipe tumbling down to the ground, with Ric landing on top of him. Embarrassed that he might have hurt Felipe by being careless, Ric said he was sorry and offered to help him up.

"Let me check out his injuries before you help him up, Ric—I want to be sure there aren't any broken bones," Eddy said.

Felipe seemed to be in a lot of pain, and the sight of his torn, bloody pants leg caused everyone to worry that Felipe might have more than just a badly scraped knee.

Using supplies from the first-aid kit, Eddy carefully cleaned out the wound while Felipe bravely tried not to show pain as the medicine touched his scraped knee and made it sting.

Dora watched proudly as Sylvia popped open a cold pack to ease the swelling of Felipe's knee and her mom folded her jacket to make a cushion for his leg.

"I'm sure glad that Mom and Sylvia are here to help, because they make a great team!"

Where's Chico?

Since Dora's—and in fact everyone's—attention was on Felipe, Dora forgot to put on Chico's leash before they entered the cave. A small rabbit ran into the cave to hide from the storm, and Chico excitedly chased it down one of the dark passages, barking wildly. Catching a glimpse of Chico out of the corner of her eye, Dora called out, "Chico, come back here this instant!"

Mrs. Cruz shouted his name, too, and Chico hesitated briefly at the sound of their voices, but chasing the rabbit seemed like too much fun to pass up, so he kept running farther into the cave.

Without thinking, Dora started after him, but she stopped when Eddy warned her, "Stop, Dora, you can't go after Chico all by yourself—it's too dangerous."

"Eddy's right, Dora," said Mom as she put her arm around Dora's shoulder. "Let's think about what we should do."

"Dora," Eddy explained gently, "remember that this cave is not Great Cavern, the cave we were planning to explore. There are no well-lit trails, we don't have a map to follow, and we just don't know what lies beyond this entrance, so I can't possibly let you chase after Chico on your own."

Already thinking about all the dangers that Chico might run into, Dora found her eyes filling with tears, and she blinked rapidly in an unsuccessful attempt to prevent them from flowing down her cheeks.

Terribly frightened for Chico, Dora and Mom kept shouting his name, but no familiar bark—in fact, no sound at all—could be heard from the cave's dark passageways. Suddenly, Dora sat down on the floor of the cave entrance, feeling completely helpless. She had broken her promise about taking care of Chico. Why hadn't she put on his leash when they ran into the cave?

Never would her family trust her again if she didn't find Chico. She could tell that Mom was disappointed with her, even though she didn't say it, and Sylvia would no longer think of her as her favorite cousin but only as a careless child.

Although Eddy felt Dora's sadness, he knew that he had to think of the entire group's safety, so he began planning their next move. He knew that as long as they all stayed together at the cave's entrance, everyone would probably be safe—everyone except Chico, of course, whose fate might not be as good. And Felipe's knee was continuing to swell—he needed medical attention and he needed it soon. Also, there was a chance that the cave might flood if the pounding rain didn't stop soon, so they absolutely couldn't just sit and wait to be rescued.

One Plan . . .
Two Plans

Finally Eddy said in a calm voice, "I have a plan, but we all have to work together. Since I have the most caving experience, I'll take Dora and Ric to look for Chico. Mrs. Cruz, will you stay here with Sylvia and the others? I'll leave one walkie-talkie with you, and maybe you can make contact with the ranger station after the storm lets up."

Mrs. Cruz started to answer Eddy, but Sylvia interrupted, "It's a good plan, Eddy, but I have a plan, too. My aunt will stay here, but I'm going for help. The ranger station isn't that far, and this storm could go on for hours. We can't wait that long to be rescued."

"Sylvia, isn't it too dangerous to go for help alone?" asked Mrs. Cruz.

"Your aunt is right—the storm is violent and there could also be flooding outside the cave," added Eddy.

"I'll stay on high ground and be very careful, and besides, *Tía* Rosita, you have to stay with Felipe, and Eddy has to help Dora find Chico," Sylvia replied.

"But Sylvia, what if it's too late for Chico and something terrible has already happened to him?" asked Dora in a frightened voice.

"He could have been bitten by a snake or some other animal," suggested Lucy.

"Or what if he can't see in the dark cave and falls into a pit?" asked Ric.

"Now stop right there," ordered Sylvia. "Chico is a small, bright dog who is pretty fast and could probably outrun most animals, and I'm sure that right now he is trying to find his way back to us."

"Sylvia could be right," Eddy said encouragingly. "Let's try her plan—it just might work."

They all nodded their heads in agreement, though they were still afraid and worried about Chico, Felipe, and now Sylvia.

"Mrs. Cruz and I both have walkie-talkies," said Eddy. "When the storm eases up, the ranger station will be able to pick up our signal, and we can tell them where we are and that Sylvia is on her way to the station."

After Sylvia put on her hooded jacket, she checked to make sure her flashlights worked, and she waved a good-bye to the group.

"Wish me luck," she said as she went out into the storm.

Standing nervously in the shadowy cave entrance, the rest of the group suddenly heard weird flapping sounds echoing up from the cave chambers, and they looked around, sensing one another's growing fear. Trembling slightly, Dora reached for her mother and squeezed her hand tightly. "What was that?" she whispered anxiously.

Immediately, Eddy took a flashlight from his backpack, saying in a comforting voice, "Don't worry. Let's all take a deep breath to calm down before Dora, Ric, and I start our search for Chico."

They tried to relax because they all knew that there was important work to do.

"There are some rules that we must follow to make our search successful," announced

Eddy. "The most important thing is that we stay together. Even though I'm not familiar with this particular cave, I have explored many caves, so please stay close to me and follow my directions. If any of us gets especially tired or confused, all three of us will head back to the cave entrance together. Mrs. Cruz will stay with Lucy and Felipe, and she and I will use the walkie-talkies to stay in touch. Any questions?"

"Dora, be very careful," whispered Mrs. Cruz, hugging Dora tightly. Secretly she didn't want to let Dora out of her sight, but she knew that Dora felt responsible for Chico running away, and she trusted that Eddy would take good care of Dora and Ric.

Mrs. Cruz and Eddy checked their walkie-talkies, flashlights, and extra batteries and were relieved to discover that everything was working. Now it was time for the Chico searchers to head deeper into the cave.

Searchers

Not knowing what to expect in this wild unexplored cave, Dora and Ric carefully followed Eddy as he walked slowly through a wide passage that appeared to be the most direct path.

"Making the right choice is very important because caves can flood, especially when the rain is nonstop. Now," he instructed Dora and Ric as he led them deeper into the cave, "turn your hard-hat headlamps on and stay close to me."

Dora's wildly active imagination painted a detailed picture of the cave flooding from the pounding rain, and all their exits getting blocked.

Ric noticed her worried look and whispered to her, "Dora, everything will be OK— I promise!"

The silence of the cave was suddenly broken by faraway barks. "I hear him—I hear Chico," shouted Dora.

Dora called out Chico's name again and again, but her shouts just echoed, bouncing back and forth through the chambers and passages of the cave.

"Eddy, where are those barks coming from? Are we following the right path?" Nervously, Dora tried to take the lead and head in the direction of Chico's barks, but Ric gently pulled her back, quietly reminding her of the rules.

27

Meanwhile Chico found out that the rabbit chase wasn't much fun because now he was cold, tired, and lonely. Terribly frightened, he barked, hoping that someone would come to his rescue, and then Chico slowly began to move forward, not knowing that he was going deeper into the cave and farther away from the search group.

While the search for Chico continued and Mrs. Cruz and Lucy waited patiently with Felipe, Sylvia was desperately trying to get back to the ranger station. She knew which trail to take, but the pouring rain made it very difficult to pick out familiar landmarks. Sylvia trudged through the mud thinking about the others in the cave. They were dry, but they had to be just as frightened as she was.

"Please let everyone be safe," Sylvia kept saying to herself, over and over.

Back in the cave, Dora calmed down just a bit and followed Eddy's lead, pushing forward even though they didn't know what lay ahead. For hours, it seemed, Dora had been listening to everyone say that everything would be OK—but would it? Then *flap, flap, flap* came that noise again.

"Turn on your flashlights," Eddy instructed, causing Dora and Ric to jump. They were entering a dark zone where the only source of light would be the beam of their flashlights and the headlights on their hats. The darkness frightened Dora, and even Ric admitted he was scared.

Walking ahead of them, Eddy stopped suddenly and stretched out his arms, showing that Dora and Ric should stop, too. As they looked along the path, which was barely visible, they saw that in just a few feet the path dropped down into a deep dark pit!

6

Bats!

Suddenly they heard a weird sound coming from the dark pit, a combination of flapping noises and high-pitched screeches. And then they saw it—an army of bats rapidly zigzagging right toward them!

Dora and Ric screamed, and Eddy reached out trying to shield them saying, "Bats won't hurt you if you don't try to hurt them, and I can tell you they'd rather have insects for dinner than human blood." Ric and Dora giggled slightly, and Eddy was glad that his attempt at humor seemed to have eased their fears.

"Mrs. Cruz to Eddy. Mrs. Cruz to Eddy. Come in, please."

Dora's and Ric's screams had been heard echoing all the way back to the cave's entrance, causing Mrs. Cruz to immediately call Eddy on the walkie-talkie, but when she got no response, she became terribly worried.

Lucy and Felipe also imagined that the worst had happened to Chico's searchers. Maybe they had fallen into a pit with no way out. Or perhaps they had been attacked by bears, coyotes, mountain lions, or snakes!

Mrs. Cruz tried to convince her group that everything was OK, but it was hard hiding her own fears. She tried again to reach Eddy on her walkie-talkie and finally heard a faint voice. "It's Eddy!" she shouted, breathing a sigh of relief.

"Eddy to Mrs. Cruz. All is fine. We just met some curious bats . . . nothing to worry about."

Dora and Ric quickly followed Eddy into another cave chamber away from the bats, an area where some light was able to come in. Bright shiny sparkles twinkled all around them, displaying hundreds of glistening stalactites. Breathless, they stood admiring the beautiful rock formations hanging down from the cave's ceiling.

"Wow! This looks like a diamond mine!" Ric said in awe.

"It's fantastic!" added Dora. "I've never seen anything so beautiful."

Then they had another surprise—a huge waterfall splashing and crashing down the wall into a lake at the end of the chamber. "A waterfall in a cave! I can't believe it!" exclaimed Dora.

When Ric jokingly suggested drinking from the lake, Eddy promptly replied, "Never drink cave water because there might be harmful acid in it, and we shouldn't get too close to the lake because we have no idea what might be lurking in or near it."

7

"We Have to Go Back"

Eddy decided to call Mrs. Cruz on the walkie-talkie and check whether everyone at the cave entrance was OK. He looked a little upset when Mrs. Cruz told him that the rain still hadn't stopped. "Dora," he said, "I'm afraid we have to go back without Chico, because it's getting late and the rain is still coming down. If the cave floods, we'll be trapped."

Dora knew that Eddy was right, but her heart ached because they hadn't found Chico. Sadly she turned to follow Eddy, but because they had been fascinated by the stalactites, they hadn't even noticed that there was another entrance to this chamber. Was this the right way? Even Eddy wasn't sure, so after studying both entrances closely, he said, "Let's all try to remember what the passage we came through looked like. Was there something special about it?"

They stood silently, trying to recall some tiny detail or clue that would help them pick the right passage.

While Eddy's small group tried to figure out which way to go, Mrs. Cruz was becoming

alarmed about rising water in one of the nearby cave passages. It seemed that the water got a little higher every time she looked. Would she and Lucy have to carry Felipe out of the cave and into the pouring rain? And she continued to worry about Dora and Chico. Eddy said everything was fine, but was he telling her the truth or just trying to make her feel better? And then there was Sylvia—had she made it back to the ranger station? So many things could have gone wrong. Why didn't the rain just stop?

Mrs. Cruz didn't want to show her concern to Lucy and Felipe, so she thought of a game they might play to keep everyone's mind off the danger that surrounded them.

"Let's play 20 Questions—I'll think of a person, place, or thing, and you two try to guess what I'm thinking about by asking me questions," Mrs. Cruz said, trying to keep her voice light. "Felipe, why don't you ask the first question?"

The small group at the cave entrance took turns asking questions and making guesses— they even laughed a few times, but the one thing they couldn't push out of their minds was the sound of the pounding rain. . . . Why didn't it just stop?

Mrs. Cruz and her group weren't the only ones worrying. Eddy knew that this much rain often caused flooding in the caves and that he had to decide which path to take—there was no more time for thinking. He chose a direction and hoped for the best.

They were moving along slowly when they approached a chamber that had several entrances, which led to separate passageways. Dora and Ric couldn't tell one rock formation from another, but Eddy examined them and explained, "We definitely came in the largest entrance, not the smallest." What he didn't know was that there had been a small rockfall since they first passed this way, changing the appearance of the entrances.

Something didn't seem quite right to Dora, so she pointed out to Eddy that, even though the entrance seemed smaller than before, in some ways the rocks looked very familiar. "Eddy, are you totally, absolutely sure that we're on the right path?"

Eddy looked down at Dora and said, "After looking carefully at the rock formations, I'm pretty sure that I've made the right choice—I wish I was absolutely sure, but either way we have to keep moving."

Another Scare

Unfortunately, they started off in the direction Eddy had chosen and walked only a few steps when, unexpectedly, rocks started falling all around them, and Eddy dropped suddenly to the ground.

"He must have been hit in the head by a rock," said an alarmed Dora, who quickly found the first-aid kit in Eddy's backpack and took out a cold pack.

"Eddy, can you hear me?" Ric asked in a high-pitched, worried voice.

Eddy slowly moved his head from side to side and moaned, "Please don't yell . . . head hurts . . ."

Eddy tried to stand up, but he felt as though the ground was spinning beneath his feet. "Don't try to move yet," warned Dora.

"Give me time . . . and I'll be . . . OK," Eddy said slowly, while Dora silently wondered whether Eddy would be able to lead them to safety.

After a few moments, Eddy said carefully, "Help me up. We have to get out of here—there might be another rockfall or even a cave-in."

They helped him stand up and got back on the trail, but Ric and Dora soon realized that Eddy was still confused when he guided them into an area blocked by fallen rocks. At that moment, Dora knew that she and Ric would have to make the decisions for a while, so they turned around and looked for a different trail.

Meanwhile back at the cave entrance, the rain was still falling, but it appeared to be letting up, and Mrs. Cruz was managing to keep Lucy and Felipe calm with the 20 Questions game. Suddenly, BANG, CRASH, BOOM echoed through the cave, scaring them into a tight huddle.

"What . . . what was that?" Lucy asked, shaken by the noise.

"I don't know," answered Mrs. Cruz, as she picked up the walkie-talkie and tried to contact Eddy.

The children stared back at her, their imaginations running wild, and every sound that they heard seemed to be louder and scarier than the one before, making them more frightened with each passing minute.

Mrs. Cruz tried again and again to call Eddy on the walkie-talkie, but there was no response, and even she started to fear for the safety of Eddy's group.

"Eddy! Eddy! Come in, please!" Still there was no response.

Staying positive and hopeful for the sake of Felipe and Lucy wasn't easy for Mrs. Cruz, but the fact that so much time had passed since they had left for Great Cavern made her think that someone must already be searching for them. Sylvia must have reached the ranger station by now, and Mrs. Cruz kept telling herself that they all would be rescued very soon.

"Please, let my daughter and Chico and everyone else be safe," she thought to herself.

It's Chico!

Deep in the cave, Eddy was feeling better, so Dora and Ric were now following his directions to get back to the entrance, when they heard *woof, woof, woof!* It wasn't an echo. It sounded real, and Dora exclaimed, "Did you hear that? It's Chico!"

Chico barked louder and louder, and Dora finally spotted a small tail sweeping back and forth between two columns. He was stuck in a very tiny passage, but his tail wagged faster and faster as Dora got closer and started talking to him, trying to assure herself and her dog that everything would be OK.

"Dora, reach in and slowly try to get him out by turning his body gently until he is free," said Eddy. "And be careful not to cause a rockfall—my head can only take so much in one day."

Dora smiled, following Eddy's directions, and soon Chico was whimpering softly and placing grateful slobbery kisses all over Dora's face.

"Oh, Chico, I'm so glad to see you. Please don't ever run away like that again," Dora scolded gently as she lovingly patted his head.

After Chico had calmed down, Dora gave him some doggie treats she had packed in her backpack, gave him a drink from her water bottle, and put on his leash.

Eddy had by now regained his strength and completely taken the lead, but Ric kept a watchful eye on him while Dora followed, holding onto Chico's leash.

Suddenly, they came to a very narrow passage that gradually sloped upward. Eddy's face glowed with hope as he exclaimed, "Great! Sometimes—just sometimes—a passage like this will lead out of the cave."

Even though Ric said he would try to get through the tight passage, it was apparent that Dora was the only one small enough to fit.

"Dora, you're very brave, but I want you to be extra careful," said Eddy. "Remember, make sure you can always reach your flashlight, because the passages will be narrow and dark, and you'll be crawling and squeezing through some very tight places. That's why some people call a passage like this a squeeze."

Dora was frightened, but she had made up her mind to find a way out for the group, so she managed to push her fears out of the way. She entered the tight passage with Chico right on her heels. After all he had been through, Dora couldn't bring herself to make Chico stay with Eddy and Ric.

It seemed to be getting darker and darker as she crawled up into the passage, and the bumpy rocks hurt her knees even through the kneepads. Chico kept so close that she could feel his breathing on the backs of her legs.

Suddenly, the squeeze became so narrow that she knew she couldn't make it much farther, and Dora realized that the only one who could possibly fit now was Chico.

At the same time, Dora saw a small speck of light in the distance. Could she be this close to getting out?

Then she had a brilliant idea. "OK, Chico, no one but you can fit through that opening, so we have to take a chance that the light means sunlight, the rain has stopped, and this passage leads out of the cave."

Chico's eyes seemed to be asking Dora what she was talking about as she pulled her special soccer medal out of her pocket. The shiny medal, which she always carried with her for luck, was the size of a quarter, and it had a picture of a soccer player on it and a pin on the back.

"Come here, Chico, and hold still," Dora said as she pinned her special soccer medal to Chico's collar. "Chico, I'm depending on you to find help. Find Mom." She held Chico up to her face kissing the top of his head while he tried to lick her face, and then she put him down in front of her, urging him up the narrow passage.

The Rescue

"Mrs. Cruz to ranger station! Please come in!" Mrs. Cruz had tried and tried to reach the ranger station since the rain had stopped.

Then suddenly she heard, "Ranger station to Mrs. Cruz. Come in."

Felipe and Lucy screamed out, "HOORAY!"

When the noise died down, Mrs. Cruz explained what was happening. A ranger told Mrs. Cruz that Sylvia had made it back to the station—she was OK and help was on its way!

Mrs. Cruz couldn't understand everything the ranger said, but she did hear that help was on its way! Now if she could only reach Eddy with the walkie-talkie and learn that his group was safe, she could finally relax.

"Mrs. Cruz to Eddy! Mrs. Cruz to Eddy! Please come in!" She was only answered by the buzzing of the walkie-talkie. The rain had finally stopped, so there shouldn't be a problem, and she knew Eddy had extra batteries. Not knowing what could have happened to the small group made her very worried. What she didn't know was that Eddy had dropped his walkie-talkie during the rockfall and it now lay under a pile of rocks.

In the squeeze, Dora began to crawl toward the light, squeezing her body tightly as she gently pushed Chico ahead of her. She was able to see a glimpse of the outside world, but she could go no farther. Remembering Eddy's instructions about how to move Chico's body to get him unstuck, she used the same method to push him through the opening now.

Pop! He was out! At first he stood at the opening in the rock and barked down at Dora—he didn't want to be separated from her again.

"Chico, Chico," she said softly, "go find Mom." He hesitated and paced around the opening, not willing to move too far from that spot, but at last she commanded firmly, "Go, Chico, go! *¡Vete!*"

A bright ray of sun suddenly shone on the soccer medal, causing it to reflect a bright light up to the rescue team flying in a helicopter not far above. They had spotted Chico!

Hearing the helicopter, Dora reached her hand through the small opening, yelling at the top of her lungs to get their attention, and Chico ran back to the opening to see if she was OK. Dora waited patiently for the rescue team to find her. On the way, the rescuers had noticed a larger cave entrance. It was now partly blocked by fallen rock, but they told Dora which direction it was, so she could find it while they removed the fallen rock. Dora crawled back to find Eddy and Ric and led them to safety as quickly as she could.

Never had Dora been so happy to see her Mom! Sylvia had come back on the helicopter with the rescue team, and their joyful shrieks were so loud that Dora could hardly hear the leader of the rescue team praising her good sense and bravery. Everyone was quiet for a moment as Felipe was carried to the helicopter, but then they knew he would be just fine when they heard him say, "See you all soon at our next cave adventure!"

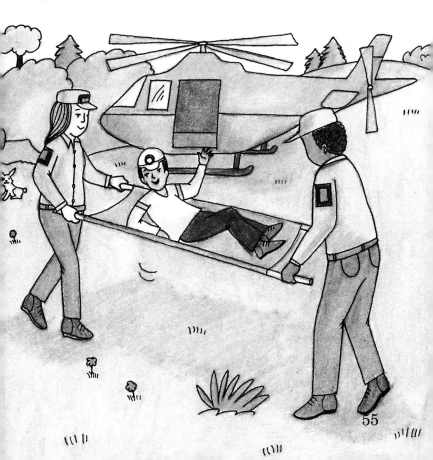

The whole group burst into laughter as they waved good-bye and turned to head back down the trail to the ranger station. Then suddenly out of nowhere, a small brown rabbit came running right across their path. Chico stopped, looked at the rabbit, and then looked up at Dora, who warned, "Don't you dare chase that rabbit, Chico!"

This time, Chico listened.